Big Ben

by Frankie Hartley
illustrated by Lesley Breen Withrow

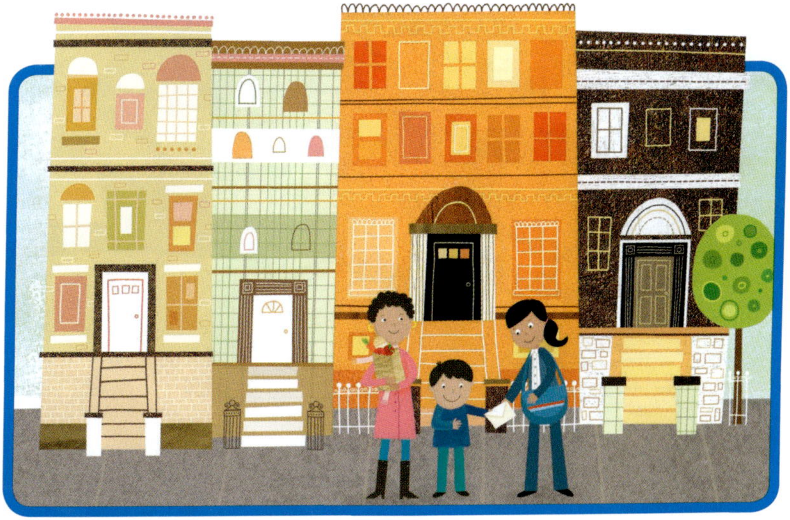

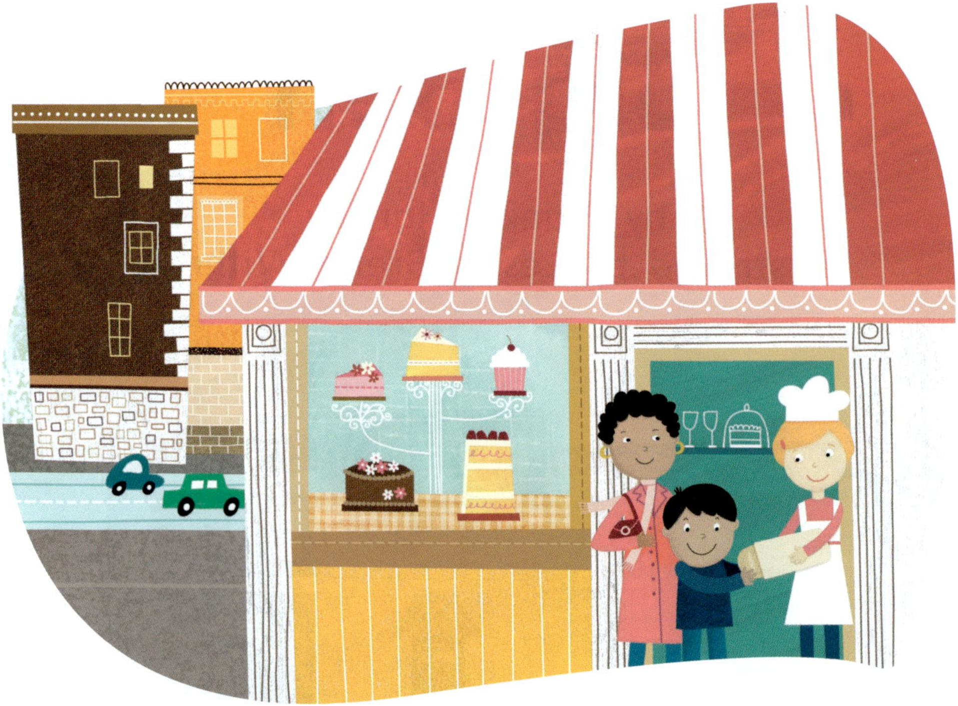

Ben likes big 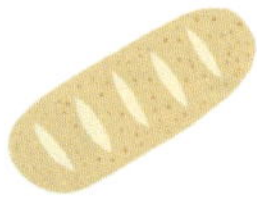 bread.

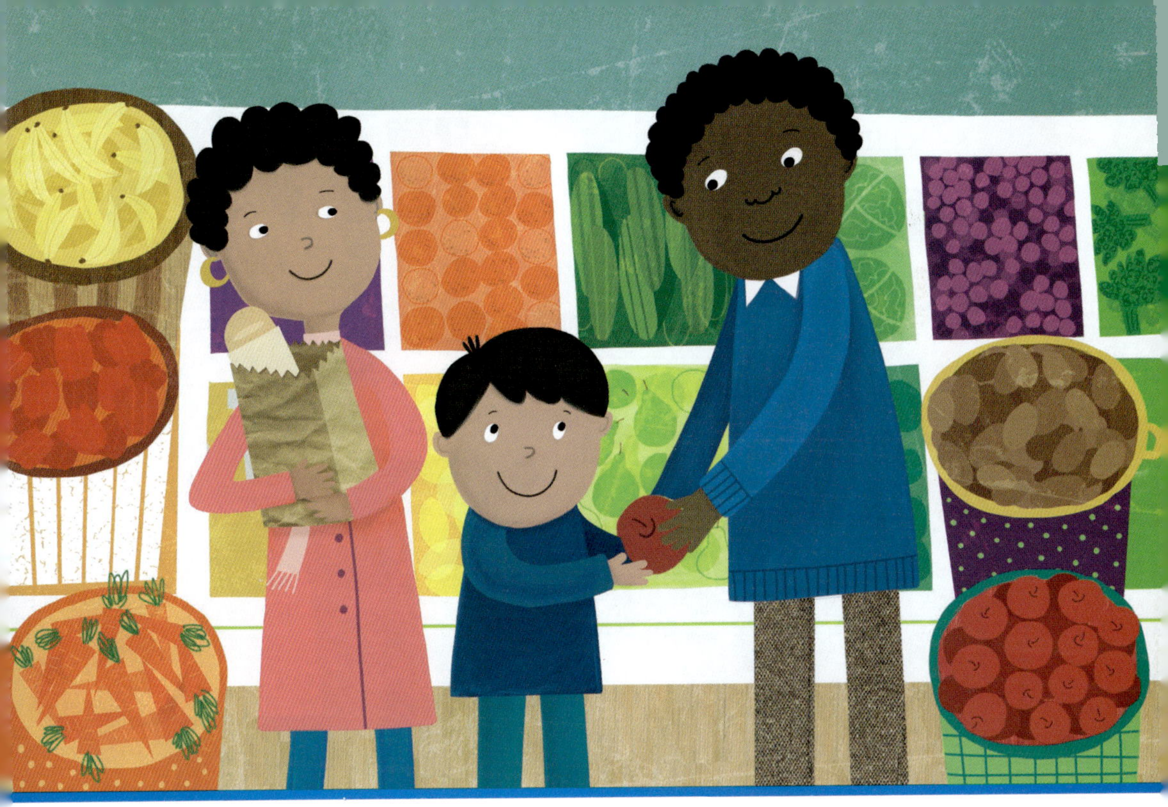

Ben likes big  apples.

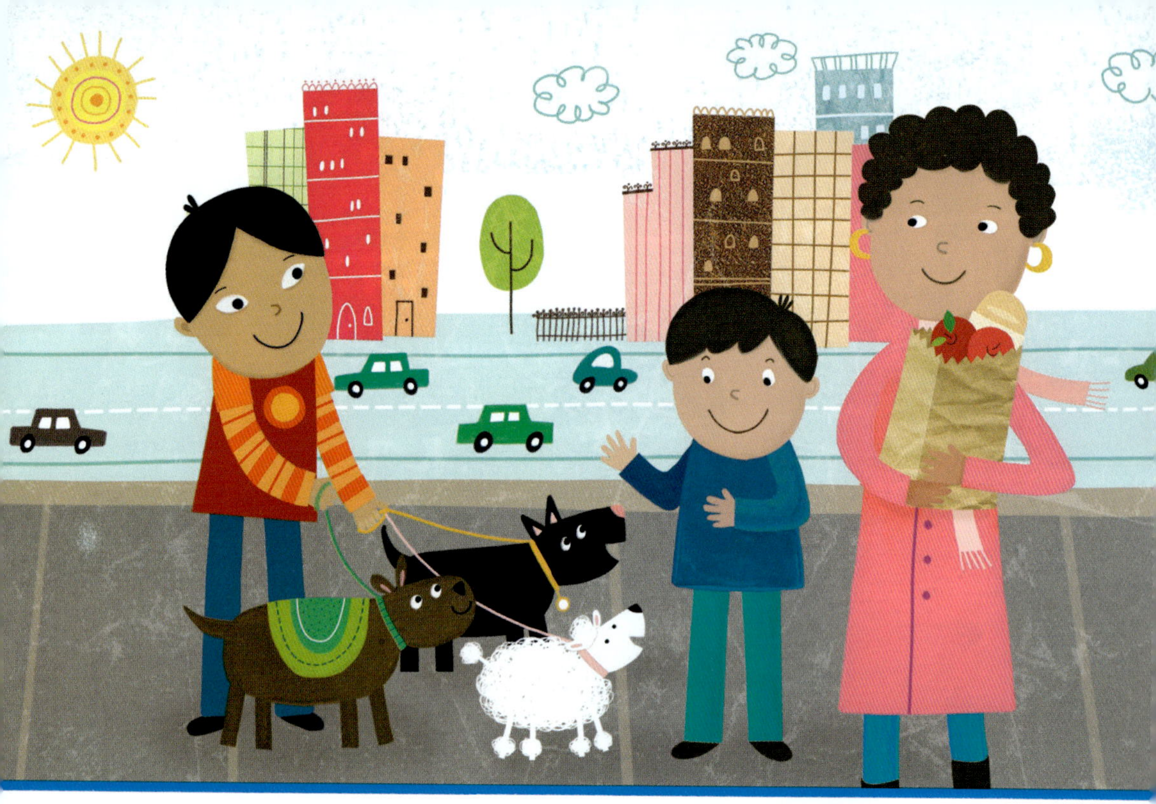

Ben likes big 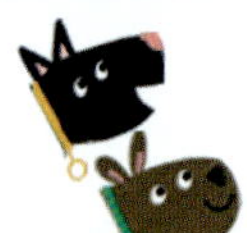 dogs.

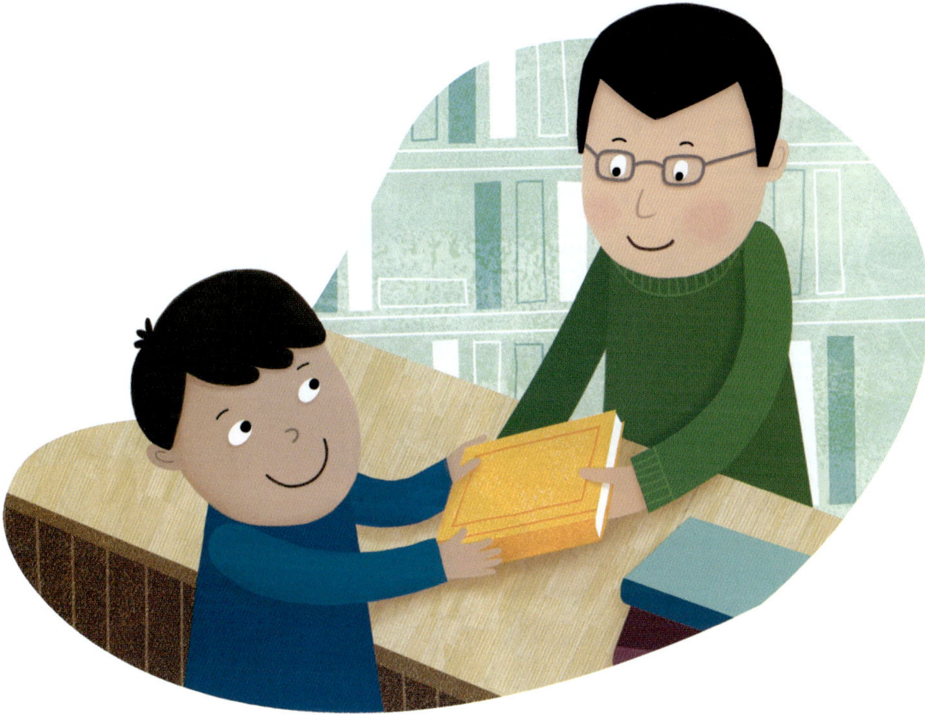

Ben likes big 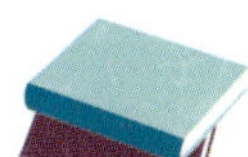 books.

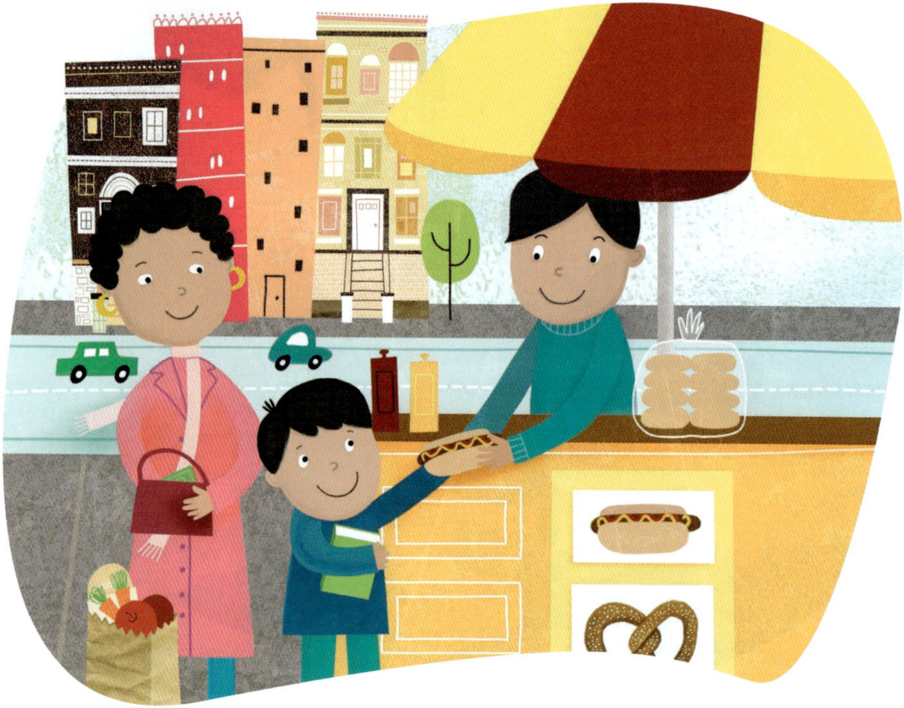

Ben likes big 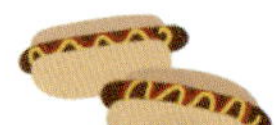 hot dogs.

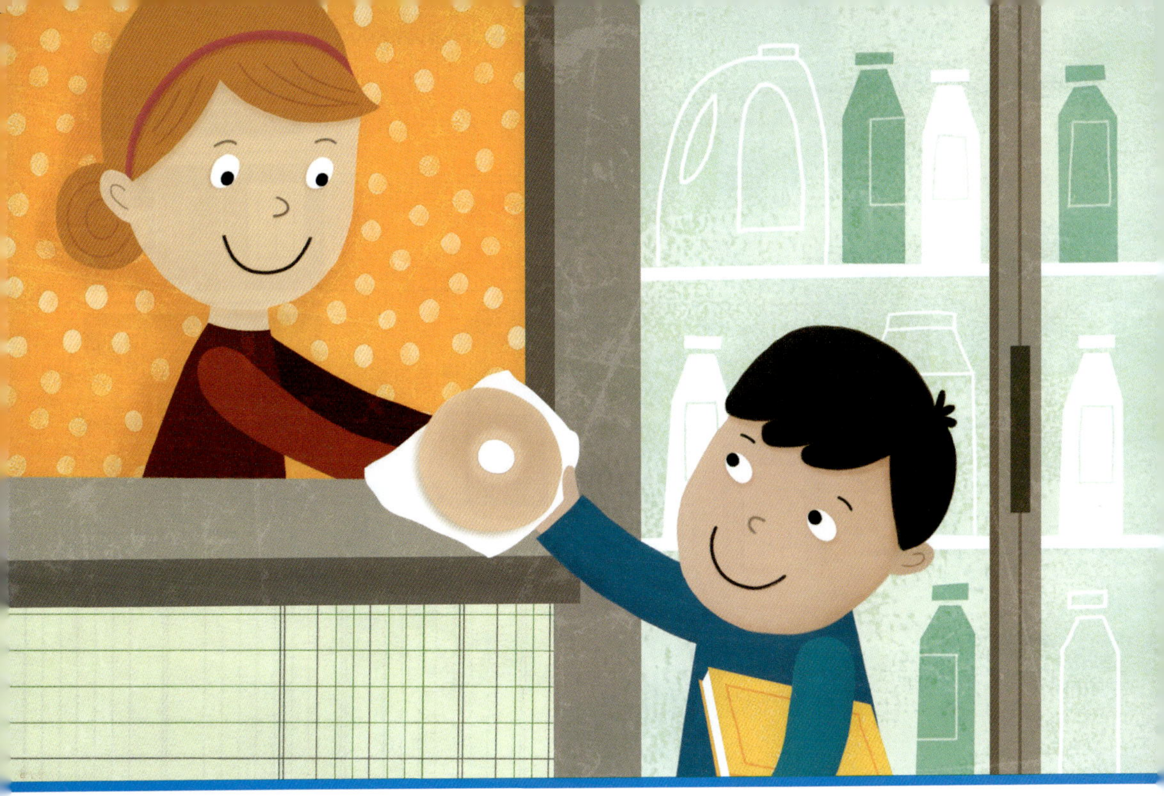

Ben likes big 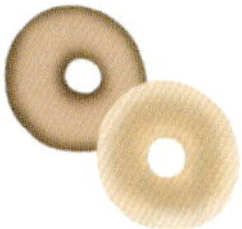 bagels.

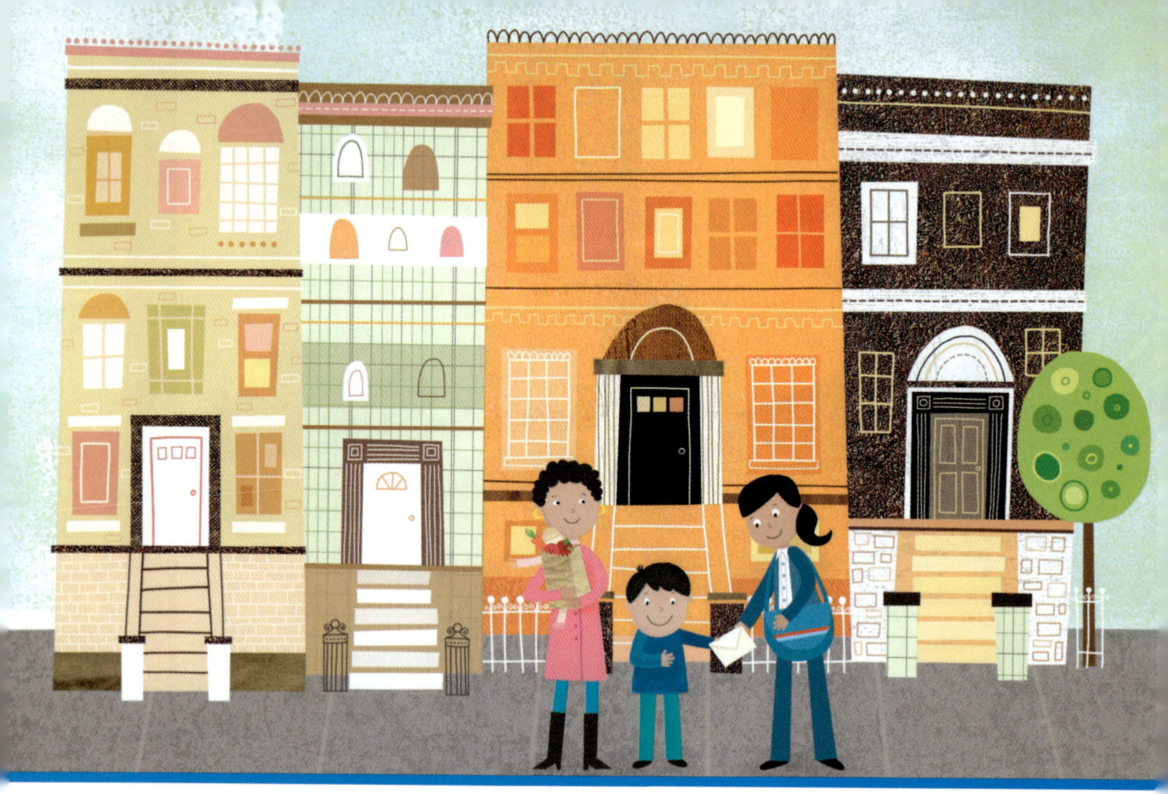

Ben is a big 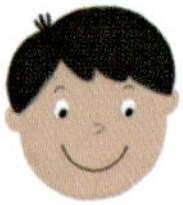 boy.